Dear Ruth,

It was meeting you.
Thank you for your help
in Die Mauberflöte

I hope you enjoyed your visit
to Los Angeles and I hope I
will see you again.

Best wishes,
Chip Resos

LOS ANGELES

LOS ANGELES

Introduction by
RAY BRADBURY

Photography by
CRAIG AURNESS, BILL ROSS & WEST LIGHT

**SKYLINE
PRESS**

Produced by Roger Boulton Publishing Services, Toronto
Designed by Fortunato Aglialoro

© 1984 Oxford University Press (Canadian Branch)
SKYLINE PRESS is a registered imprint of Oxford University Press

ISBN 0-19-540601-X
1 2 3 4 – 7 6 5 4
Printed in Hong Kong by Scanner Art Services, Inc., Toronto

I ONLY DO IT TO ANNOY,
BECAUSE I KNOW IT TEASES

a provocation by Ray Bradbury

Do what, to annoy and tease whom?

Cry 'salaam', 'hallelujah' and 'gloria' to Los Angeles, thereby causing millions of enraged peasants in Chicago, Detroit, New York and Washington, D.C. to throw themselves to the earth, writhing in ecstasies of envy and malice.

That has been my business for some years now: to provoke and enrage those mobs who show up on our California doorstep to torch the castle, but stay on for blithe tiffins with the Monster.

The Monster is, of course, Los Angeles, and I am a Child of the Beast, its chief critic, but its staunch defender.

Before you hurl this book across the room, and then yourself fall frothing to the floor, already tried beyond endurance, let me give you a few examples of how I have intuited Los Angeles and its tourist drop-ins in the past.

A New York editor friend, intellectual art critic and part-time snob, arrived here some twenty years ago, to unpack his suitcase of sneers, and paste on his mask of opprobrium. Nothing pleased him. There was no theatre, no food, no city, nothing. In the words of the old 'Two Black Crows' recording, even if it was good he wouldn't like it. 'Corruption,' he cried, 'thy name is Los Angeles!'

'Yes,' I replied, 'and we will, in time, corrupt you. Now hear this: one year from now, you will wake at dawn to find yourself in a Bing Crosby sports shirt, all bleeding hibiscus, as you tool along our palm-lined avenues in an open sports car, wiggling your Mickey Mouse ears.'

That dawn, needless to say, came not a year later, but within six months. Hearing a glad shout one day, I glanced up to see my friend, thoroughly corrupted, dyed by the sun, inhabiting both sports shirt and open MG, waving as he rushed by to become part of the Cinerama wallpaper of Hollywood.

When the Emperor Hirohito arrived in Los Angeles I saw him being driven by limousine into the Beverly Wilshire Hotel courtyard. I waved, and the Emperor waved back, as I muttered:

'Bet you twenty he's just visited Disneyland!'

That night, there was the Emperor, on TV, lost in Anaheim, shaking hands with the Mouse.

I have a formula for handling Easterners who arrive with rusty starch in their shirts and bloodstreams. I give them the L.A. Tour, but end the day at Disneyland, on the Mark Twain steamboat at nine p.m., with a Dixieland Band marching the Saints as fireworks rebuild the sky.

The starch vanishes and a most peculiar smile begins to grow around the mouths of my tourist friends.

When François Truffaut, the French film director of *400 Blows* and *Jules and Jim*, first arrived here he asked me to give him a brief but brilliant tour.

'What,' I asked my wife in a panic, 'should I show François to

(above) William Hogarth: *Some of ye principal inhabitants of ye Moon, as they were perfectly discovered by a telescope brought to ye greatest perfection since ye last eclipse. 1724.*

knock him *quiche* over *cognac*?'

'The Hollywood Hills,' my wife replied. 'At night, the view of Los Angeles. Are we or are we not the new City of Light?'

We took Truffaut up to stare at 400 square miles of stars strewn in every direction.

Those lights, that city, is in this book.

What next? Twenty years ago, one of the grandest supermarkets in all the world existed here. Listen to its name: 'The Piggly-Wiggly Continental'. A food and wine emporium of such variety, imagination and beauty that supermarkets like it spread out across the country to change our land and move on through the world.

How did Truffaut react to our midnight landscape and noontime supermarket? With his cinematographer's eyes he scanned the vast Andromeda Nebula sprawl of our town, and gave a proper shout of joy. When the Piggly-Wiggly Continental inundated him with its sights, sounds and smells, he ran like a boy through a toyshop on Christmas Eve, buying things to mail home.

All of which begins to tell you *what* about Los Angeles?

We did not invent the light bulb nor the illuminated city, but we did do a great job of squashing flat the biggest damn Christmas tree on earth, then spreading it out to carpet 80 community-towns, 80 oranges in search of a navel.

There *is* no navel, of course. Los Angeles doesn't really exist. But so far, no one has noticed. Back to that later . . .

What we *did* invent was the supermarket, and sent it forth like a glorious neon-fruitcake-Patton-tank to conquer the world. The Piggly-Wiggly, as I was saying earlier, has invaded Europe and will one day lap, flood, drown, and revolutionize Russia, no matter how she shrieks, hides, or tries to beat us off with the *Communist Manifesto*.

The sweetly gross materials of our Grocery Pig, grown larger than libraries, will do more than Marx and Milton can to explain Mankind to Man.

We will, in sum, creep under the Iron Curtain on our bellies and rise up to sell soapsuds, coke, computers, and those nicely-rounded warm Levi buns that are so pinchable—these last, as you well know, invented only here in Los Angeles.

I am reminded of a night in Paris, five years back. It was the evening before Bastille Day. Staring from my hotel window around ten o'clock, I turned to my wife and cried: 'My God! there are 100,000 Angelenos jumping to that rock music down in the square! I came to France to see Frenchmen, not *them*!'

Curious, I went downstairs.

What did I find?

Not California Angelenos at all. But 100,000 French lads and lasses *dressed* like Angelenos!

We have conquered the world and no one has noticed. Not even our own politicians.

For, you see, the true revolutions of the world are not political but psychological, influenced by weather which changes custom which invents arts, clothing, and communication.

It follows then that we are greater revolutionaries than Marx ever dreamed of as he wiped the remnants of cheesecake from his beard. For we have invented a lot of living here, or near here, in Los Angeles.

The men from our Muscle Beach in Santa Monica inhabit the Conan/Goliath/Hercules papier mâché and pasta films of Italy and beyond. Our surfers, borrowing the paddleboard from Hawaii, have sported in the minds and tuned the songs of two generations.

We shovel in jetloads of singers and lyric writers from the docktowns of England, but they all record, live, and bank here.

It follows that we control a good portion of the recording

industry, films, television, radio, and the tape cassette business from here. By all means, give us your praise.

We invented the orange. Or, rather, reinvented it and all the other mania health foods with which we grew larger artichokes, tennis players, football stars, and Olympic swimmers, and made them taller, meaner, and better than most of the bounders, leapers, and grunters of the world. Along the way, with our nutrition, we also reinvented the Japanese, magnifying them from 5'5" compacts into six foot gameplayers on their way to a slam-dunk.

Most of the world's greatest composers live here, or have lived here at one time or another. By living composer today we mean, of course, the film-score artist-conductor, the bright bastard son out of *E.T.* by *Close Encounters*. Our science fiction film-scores move to sound-pollute (if you wish) or air-condition us with tonal delights in the Hollywood Bowl and thence float east across Africa to Japan.

When the world thinks of the technological revolutions handed it by the United States, it thinks only briefly of New York, still more briefly of Washington, D.C.,—for the true capital of our country is Los Angeles, or Hollywood as we sometimes call it.

The winter White House, with most of the past five Presidents, has been located a few miles east or a few miles south of L.A. By the year 2083, since you ask me for predictions, there will be a permanent White House in Palm Springs. Twenty years from now, when Walter Annenberg moves out, Maureen Reagan will move in.

By then we will have taken over and dominated all of the communications industries, the banks, publishing and,—just look at the Napa Valley grow,—wine! That's stretching the City Limits of L.A. a trifle, but we're talking California here, a varietal tongue of Los Angeles.

Not long after 1984, most of the world will be California or Los Angeles oriented. I say this not only to bow to truth, but like the bad boy I claim to be in my title—to tease and annoy.

It's all a bit incredible, seeing as how we do indeed have no navel. Slouching towards L.A. it seems as if the centre cannot hold. There is no intelligentsia, no hierarchy, no clique of snobs, no gangs of six or ten or twelve who direct literary or music or watercolor traffic and bruise you with their batons if you don't obey. That is what makes us so attractive—that fact that we are really free and can do—or *almost* do—as we wish, in ten dozen fields. Our ideas, free to fly or to be shot down, will go on moving to restructure a waiting world. And we'll do it all while directing it all with a sunburnt beak from a surfboard.

Will we have no mercy on the world? None. Will we love every minute of taking over and controlling those pale, long-nosed arrogant Manhattanites? We will. Will they forgive us as they slip into their bikinis and slap on the noon lotions? They will. Will the world be a better place because we have made it a lovely ruin? Indeed. Because we are already busy rebuilding ourselves, in some ways closer to the better parts and things in Rome, Paris, and London. Half-barbarian, we will not stay that way.

The wave of the Future, irrefutable, indomitable, irreversible, is to be found lodged in our sunlit hightide tv aerial, rock-and-roll flood space symphony video cassette environment.

The name of it all is Los Angeles. And one day, if it finally decides that it must *truly* function, the United Nations will move here.

There. Have I annoyed, teased, and irritated *everyone*? Dear Lord, I hope so!

Los Angeles, August 1983   RAY BRADBURY

1 Harbor Freeway, Los Angeles

2 Mission San Gabriel Arcángel (founded 1771, church 1791-1805), San Gabriel

3 *(right)* Point Dume, north of Malibu

4 *(left)* Convento (1806), Mission San Fernando Rey de España (founded
1797), northwest of San Fernando

5 San Bernadino Freeway, looking west at sunset, Los Angeles

6 *(left)* Theme Building and Restaurant
Los Angeles International Airport

7 General view of Los Angeles Basin from
Griffith Park

8 Santa Monica Freeway, looking west at sunset

9 *(right)* Downtown after an unusual winter storm, looking towards the San Gabriel Mountains

10 Santa Anita Race Track

11 *(right)* International track and field event, 3,000 metre race, Los Angeles Coliseum

12 Mexican dancing, Olvera Street, downtown Los Angeles

13 Botanical Gardens, Huntington Library

14 Hollywood Freeway, looking west, with Hollywood on the left

15 *(right)* The Colossus at Magic Mountain, largest wooden
roller-coaster ever built, 9,200 feet tall, with speeds up to 65 mph

16 *(left)* Hollywood Reservoir, Hollywood
Hills

17 Century City complex, off Santa
Monica Boulevard. Planned by Alcoa
Corporation on the site of the former 20th
Century Fox Studios; shopping centre built
during 1950's; Century City Hotel designed
by Minoru Yamasaki, built 1966

18 *(left)* Heavy surf at Malibu

19 Farmers' Market, Fairfax district; famous for fresh produce, vegetable and citrus stands

20 Wilshire Boulevard near Western

21 *(right)* Santa Monica, looking north to Ocean Boulevard

22 Early evening on Santa Monica Pier

23 Yacht basin, Marina del Rey

24 *(left)* Santa Monica Freeway and Harbor Freeway interchange, looking northeast

25 Wilshire Boulevard at Vermont Street

26 Santa Monica Pier at dusk

27 'Fisherman's Village', Marina del Rey; specialty shops and restaurants
overlooking the Marina Channel

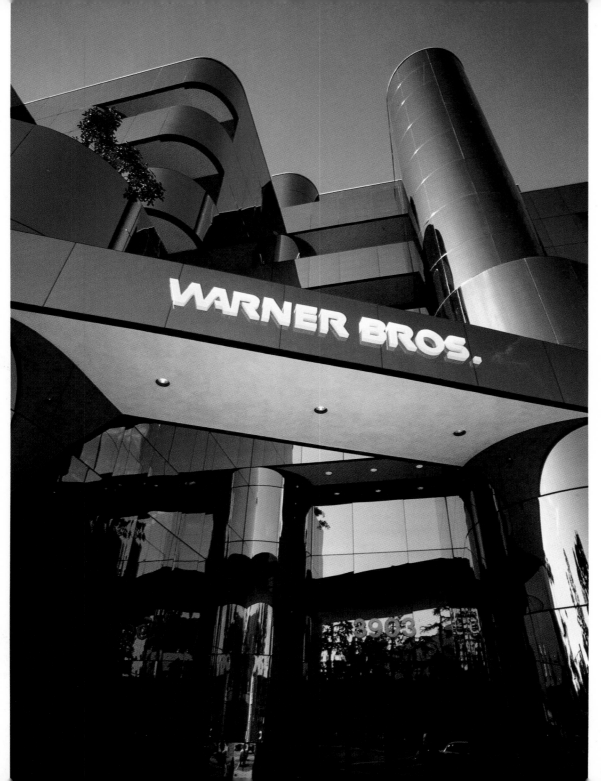

28 Warner Brothers office building,
Burbank, originally founded 1919

29 Hollywood Hills, with metal sign 50 feet high, originally built 1923, restored 1981

30 Mural of Clark Gable and Carol Lombard outside Mann's Chinese Theatre, Hollywood

31 *(right)* Olympic Velodrome Cycling Site, California State College, Dominguez Hills

32 *(left)* Annual New Year's Day Tournament of Roses Parade, Pasadena

33 Mann's Chinese Theatre, setting of many Hollywood premieres

34 Malibu Colony looking north; home of many famous personalities

35 (right) Beverly Hills

36 Rodeo Drive, Beverly Hills, with the
Beverly Wilshire Hotel in the background

37 *(right)* Malibu Pier

38 Comedy screen test, Universal City, site of Universal Studios

39 Universal City, Universal Studios

40 Bradbury Building (1893)

41 *(right)* Plaza Pasadena, shopping mall near the Pasadena Civic Center on Green Street

42 *(left)* 'Ice Capades', Long Beach

43 Space Shuttle, built by North American Rockwell, in
Palmdale assembly area before being taken to testing facilities at
Edwards Air Force Base in the Mojave Desert

44 *(left)* Hollywood Bowl Amphitheater, with Frank Lloyd Wright concert shell (1924–28)

45 Music Center for the performing arts (1964–61); the Dorothy Chandler Pavilion, designed by Welton Becket and Associates (finished 1969)

46 *(left)* Beverly Hills

47 Henry E. Huntington Library and Art Gallery (1919)

48 *(left)* Griffith Park Observatory
and Planetarium

49 Bonzai Festival, West Los Angeles
Buddhist Church

50 Olympic Track and Field Award Ceremony, Los Angeles Coliseum

51 Judges and officials, Los Angeles Coliseum

52 Copy of Michelangelo's 'David', Forest Lawn Memorial Park, Glendale

53 *(right)* Getty Museum, near Pacific Palisades, Malibu, housing the Paul Getty collection and modeled on the Villa dei Papyri in Herculaneum

54 *(left)* Pacific Palisades, looking
southwest

55 Hale House, Heritage Square; a 'Queen
Anne' Eastlake house (c. 1888)

56 George C. Page Museum of La Brea
Paleontological Discoveries (opened 1977)
La Brea Tar Pits

57 *(right)* Bonaventure Hotel, downtown
Los Angeles; designed by John Portman
(1977–78)

58 *(left)* Josiah Royce Hall, University of California, Los Angeles; one of the buildings of the 1929 quadrangle, designed by Allison and Allison

59 Biltmore Hotel, downtown Los Angeles; designed by Schultze and Weaver (1923)

60 Los Angeles skyline at sunset

61 *(right)* Movie-making, Los Angeles

62 Heart of downtown Los Angeles

63 First Methodist Church of Hollywood,
Franklin and Highland ; Original Church
(1933) destroyed by fire and rebuilt (1936)
by architects Douglas McLellan and
Allen McGill

64 *(left)* Evening picnic on Malibu Beach

65 Ungaro-Emmanuel's, exclusive women's clothing store, Rodeo Drive, Beverly Hills

66 *(left)* Los Angeles County Museum of
Art (est. 1965); Armand Hammer Wing

67 Venice Beach

68 *(left)* City Hall, Los Angeles; built
(1926–28) by Austin, Parkinson, Martin
and Whittlesey; with 27 stories the only
building over 13 stories high until 1957

69 CNA Building and First Congregational
Church; 'high-tech' mirror-glass office
building designed 1972; English Gothic
style church across the street on Sixth and
Commonwealth built 1932

70 Queen Anne's Cottage, Los Angeles
Arboretum, designed by A.A. Bennett.
'Lucky' Baldwin owned this as a guest
house from 1875–1909

71 *(right)* Mural painted on ceiling of
Bullock's Wilshire in 1929 by Herman
Sachs

72 Century City, Century Towers; Century
Plaza Towers designed by Minoru
Yamasaki—part of the ABC Entertainment
Center

73 *(right)* Santa Monica, looking east

74 Los Angeles Dodgers Stadium (1962), Chavez Ravine

75 *(right)* Century City and Santa Monica Boulevard at dusk

76 *(left)* Poppies and other wildflowers in Antelope Valley

77 Santa Monica and Venice Beach, from the Santa Monica Pier

78 Snow on Kratka Ridge, San Gabriel Mountains

79 Santa Monica Beach

80 *(left)* Sunset over Santa Monica
Mountains State Park, between Malibu
and the San Fernando Valley

81 *Conan the Barbarian*, live theater
production, Universal City, Hollywood

82 The *Queen Mary*, former Cunarder and
once the world's largest passenger liner
afloat, in dock at Long Beach since 1967

83 *(right)* Los Angeles by night

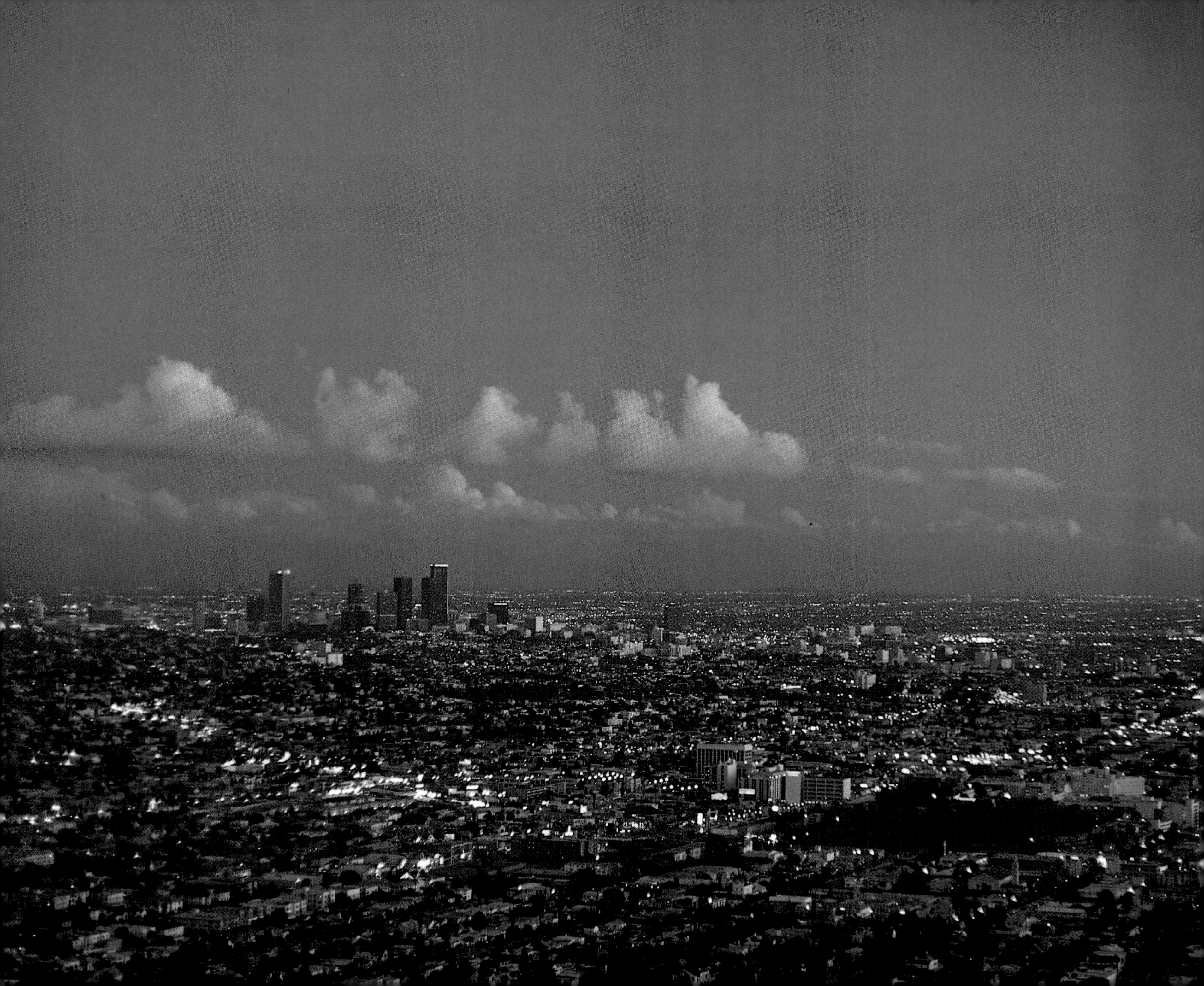

84 *(left)* Marina del Rey

85 Santa Monica Beach and Pier after storm

86 New moon over the city

PHOTOGRAPHIC CREDITS

CRAIG AURNESS 1, 2, 4, 5, 7–9, 12, 14, 16, 17, 19, 21–30, 33–37, 39, 40, 43–46, 48, 49, 52–54, 58, 66–69, 72, 73, 77, 79, 83, 84; BILL ROSS 3, 10, 11, 13, 18, 20, 31, 32, 38, 41, 47, 50, 51, 55, 57, 59, 63, 70, 71, 75, 76, 78, 81, 85, 86; CHARLES O'REAR 42, 61, 64, 80; PIERRE KOPP 6, 65, 82; LARRY LEE 15, 74; FUKUHARA PHOTOGRAPHY INC. 56; GENE STEIN 62; WILLIAM JAMES WARREN 60